TO FORGIVE THE
UNFORGIVABLE

First Published 1997

Other books by Stephen Morris include:

Lord of Death (Play)
Alien Poets
Penny Farthing Madness
Born Under Leo
The Revolutionary
The Kingfisher Catcher
Death of a Clown
The Moment of Truth
Too Long at the Circus
Rolling Dice

Children's Stories
The Umbrellas of Mr Parapluie

Published by the Moving Finger
PO Box 2923
Warley
West Midlands
B67 5AG
England.

British Library Cataloguing-in-publication Data.
A catalogue for this book is available from the British Library.

Copyright © 1997

TO FORGIVE THE UNFORGIVABLE

By
STEPHEN MORRIS

THE
MOVING
FINGER

CREATIVE WRITING PROMOTIONS

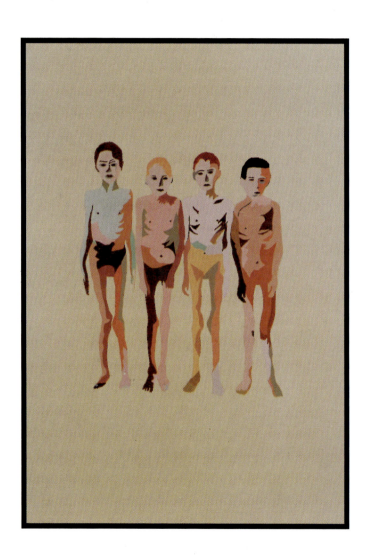

TO FORGIVE THE UNFORGIVABLE

Just over two years ago I visited the two camps Auschwitz-Birkenau in Poland. Even though I had been prepared for the silent horror of it all I was still shocked. It was perhaps something to do with fear, a lack of comprehension or being unable to understand what had actually occurred in my own life time. It does seem that I have always known what happened in that period of history. The newsreels I saw as a child when the camps were liberated at the end of the second world war. The numerous films such as 'Judgement at Nuremburg', 'The Pawnbroker', 'Sophie's Choice', and more recently, 'Schindler's List'. as well as the masses of literature I have absorbed on the subject, must all have had their effect. But this enormously successful experiment in mass extermination, which took place at Auschwitz-Birkenau, evades almost every adjective to describe it. I have tried with words and images to express my feelings, to capture some of the blind terror, the revulsion and the sheer repugnance of it all and it has been difficult.

As with the words, I have kept the paintings simple as well as approaching the subject surrealistically. Above all I have tried to create images that will linger in the memory. The initial vision is a blast of colour but within that there are individual pieces of tragedy, pain, suffering and death. All, though, it is not hopeless. There is a tomorrow and that may be better. One's faith in human beings may be shaken but not entirely lost. This episode in the history of mankind should be taken as a warning and that is another reason for the exhibition. We must not forget the evil that man can do and we must always be on our guard.

The title of the exhibition has been changed many times during the two years I have worked on it. It is not for me to tell anyone to forgive the unforgivable, I am not Jewish nor did I lose anyone however indirectly. I do however, feel a great pity and a deep sadness for humanity, mainly for the victims but also in an odd way for the perpetrators.

We must never forget the unforgettable for the sake of all those who were consumed in the Holocaust. It is perhaps another cry from the dead to the living. A further plea in the struggle for human rights, for equality, tolerance, liberation and justice. Above all, it is a shout for goodness and decency with which to blow away the black cloud, created by the Holocaust, that still hangs over the twentieth century.

Stephen Morris
1997

How to answer the unanswerable
To question the unquestionable
To explain the inexplicable
How to accept the unacceptable
To tolerate the intolerable
and....
How to forgive the unforgivable
Which we may
And to forget the unforgettable
Which we shall not

Could one forgive, or one forget
The storm that took their lives away
Their cries for mercy and for life
No, not for a second, minute, hour or day
Not for a month, a year, a decade, or two,
So deeply wounded, the scars will stay

A quiet rules, a silence reigns
For the dead cannot cry again
They'll not smile nor love nor hate
Their fire will never turn to flame
They will not scream, nor will they shout
For the lifeless feel not their pain

The tyrants ruled, the master race
Their 'special' treatment to bequeath
Systemised, ordered, concise and neat
Hair, fat, skin and golden teeth
To utilized toward their goal
Their only garland, a barb wired wreath

No sunrise for the millions dead
The madness no excuse for sin
Love of orders, question not
Obey the rules, the Nazi doctrine
"Follow the Fuhrer", "Follow the Fuhrer"
So easy, so cosy, what discipline.

The names of the concentration camps somehow hold within them an unspeakable and horrendous terror, especially those which were used for extermination. Treblinka, Chelmo, Ravensbruck, Buchenwald, Belsen, Dachau, Sobibor, Majdanek, Mauthausen, Belsec and Stuttof. But from the very heart of Europe the names Auschwitz-Birkenau will be forever carved on the history of mankind.

Trucks they came from everywhere
To bring old, young, the gypsy and the Jew
The infirmed, insane and crippled too
To join a grotesque and decisive queue
The final solution, the official plan
Dear God, such disgrace to each and every man

When a child dies there is a loss
The loss of infinite possibility, of the chance
To recreate, to discover, to achieve
To learn, to play, even to dance
But a million died,
Murdered in an act of genocide

Crematorium smoke clawed for the sky
Signalling to each they would have to die
Not on some battlefield or soft death bed
But choking out life to join the pitiable dead
Chambers of gas and Zyclone B
An atrocity to shame our history

The odour of death hanging in the air
Torture, hatred and misery everywhere
The smouldering fear on every face
This incredibly to destroy a race
It was they said to purify
So innocent millions had to die

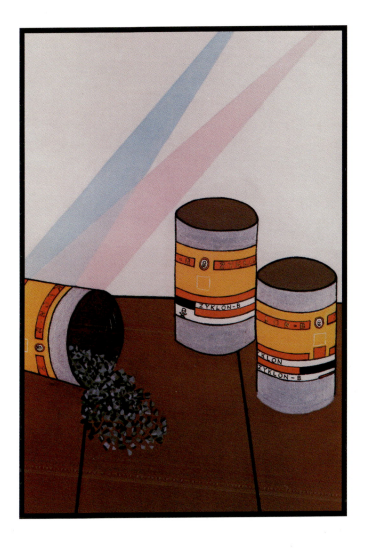

When a nation allows violence and evil to dominate its thinking, its behaviour and its imagination – anything can happen – and it did.

A state to destroy the soul
Twisting dreams to useless dust
Belief abandoned turned into stone
Brother, comrade, friend, not one to trust
No light, nor hope, from David's star
Only desolation and dark disgust

Mengales hand, the hand of God
To the right for life the left for death
But come special children you can be saved
It need not be your final breath
Medical experiments to create a master race
All lesser people to vanish without a trace

Brutal murder became natural. It destroyed the definitions of right and wrong. The Germans killed to purify their people and the killing became normality.

And death itself came in many ways
Overwork, starvation and the hangman's rope
Phenol injections, exhaustion and fatal disease
And the chamber of gas to deny all hope
The suffering and pain what was it worth?
Only to escape a hell on earth

Soft words they come so easy
So good, so pure, so bland
Forked tongues to give the hopeless hope
With the pledge of a promised land
But the waves of slaughter continued
Directed by a Godless hand

The shame and the pity is what evil men can do from high motives. It is this that is most pernicious and savage which then enables the principles of pragmatism to prevail and what becomes useful is right.

The explanations are not too easy
For perhaps within each mans soul
An evil lurks, it waits, it hides
And will always take its toll
It must though be checked and stopped
And forever kept in control

When in free choice man elects for wrong
And if profanity rules the day
We must shout, protest and write again
Against the wrongs men do and what they say
For evil will surely flourish
When good men in their silence hide their heads away

How to answer the unanswerable
To question the unquestionable
To explain the inexplicable
How to accept the unacceptable
To tolerate the intolerable
and....
To forgive the unforgivable

ACKNOWLEDGEMENTS

Many, many thanks to the following for all their help, encouragement, advice, technical skills, interest and love in regard to the whole project including the film, the exhibition and the book.

Christiane Mauviard, Bob Roberts, Bob Wilson, Sarah Mortimer, Frank Quigg, Robert Conybeare, Stuart Daniels, Caroline Jenkinson, Andrew Lawson, Martyn Oversteegen, Dave Reeves, Justina Kaminski, Kristof Kaminski, Konrad Dadasieuilz, John Aubrey, John Mildenhall, John Sweet, Gay Lane, John Sylvester and Brian Bishop.

8 This is Steve Malone. He works for the police. He's very clever. Steve wants to find the killer.

9 Steve talks to his boss.

We don't know the killer.

No, we don't, but his name starts with 'M'.

10 The names of three men at the Uluru Hotel start with 'M'. Steve has their photos and he knows about them. He writes about them in his book.

THE PHOTOGRAPHS

STEVE'S BOOK

Eric Manton
A doctor. He works in a big hospital in Sydney.

Micky Munro
A singer. Many people in Australia and America like Micky's music.

William Mortimer
He's got a lot of big shops in Sydney and a lot of money.

Chapter 2

11 It's Saturday. Steve Malone arrives in Uluru.

12 It's very hot. Steve wants to have a swim. He puts his bag under the bed. The photos and his book are in his bag.

THE WRONG MAN

Chapter 1

1 This is Uluru. It's a big rock in Australia. It's very hot here and there isn't a lot of rain.

2 This is a big hotel near Uluru. A lot of people come to the hotel on holiday.

3 Two men are in a hotel room. They aren't on holiday. They're killers. They want to kill the Police Commissioner. The Police Commissioner is the boss of the Australian police.

> The Police Commissioner is coming on Monday.

> Yes, boss. Monday is the day.

> Have you got the gun?

> Yes, boss. I've got it here.

TO THE POL

4 A person in the hotel knows one of the men and writes a letter to the police.

5 This is Sydney. Sydney is a big town in Australia. It has a lot of tall buildings.

6 It's Friday morning. Four men are in an office in a tall building in Sydney. They work for the police.

7 This is the letter. It has no name on it.

THE POLICE
COMMISSIONER
IS COMING TO
ULURU HOTEL ON
MONDAY
M IS HERE
HE'S GOT A GUN

13 Steve comes back to his room. He finds a young woman there. She's looking at his things.

15 Steve is very angry with Sally. She has Steve's book and the photos of the three men in her hands. The book and the photos were in Steve's bag. His bag was under the bed. It was closed. Now it's on the bed and it's open.

14 Sally Peters knows about the Police Commissioner and the killer. She wants to write a story about it for her newspaper.

Sally knows about Steve. He's working for the police and she wants to help him.

16 Later, Steve and Sally are sitting in the garden of the hotel. Now Steve likes Sally. Perhaps she *can* help him.

Steve! The letter to the police! The writer of the letter knows the killer.

Yes. He's afraid and doesn't want to talk.

What are we going to do, Steve?

This evening we'll watch Manton, Mortimer and Munro.

17 Sally and Steve are eating in the hotel. They're watching the people there.

Look, Steve! There's William Mortimer. He's watching us!

And he's eating a lot of food.

18

And there's Dr Manton. Who's that gi with him? Sh isn't happy.

That's Manton's daughter, Joan.

19 Now Steve and Sally are watching Micky Munro, the singer, and his manager. Sally doesn't like Micky Munro's manager.

20 Munro's manager is angry with Sally and Steve.

Is that Micky's manager? I don't like his face. Prehaps he's the killer.

Look! He's coming to our table.

Why are you watching Micky? That makes us very angry.

OK, OK! Let's go now, Sally!

21 Steve and Sally go back to Steve's hotel room. They find a letter on the floor.

23 Steve and Sally can't understand the letter.

Look, Steve! What's that on the floor?

It's a letter!

22

M IS THE WRONG MAN

Why 'the wrong man'? Who is writing these letters?

I don't know, but I'm going to find him. Perhaps the killer wants to find him, too!

7

Chapter 3

24

SUNDAY
MORNING
Come and
climb
ULURU
Bus starts
at seven

25 It's Sunday morning. A hotel bus is taking people from the hotel to Uluru. They're going to climb the rock. Micky Munro is talking to his manager.

I'm going up. Are you coming?

No, I'm going to stay at the hotel. I want to write some letters.

26 Steve and Sally aren't going in the bus to Uluru. They're staying at the hotel. They're going to work.

Mortimer, Munro and Manton are all going to Uluru.

Yes, that's good! Now we can go into their rooms. Micky Munro's room first!

27 Micky Munro's manager runs into the room. He's very angry. He has a gun.

What are you doing in Micky's room? I'm going to kill you!

8

28 Steve hits the man.
The gun falls to the floor.

29 Steve and Sally are helping Munro's manager up from the floor.

30 Munro's manager talks to Steve and Sally about Micky. He's afraid for Micky.

31 'In May, Micky was in hospital in Sydney. He talked to Dr Manton and his daughter.'

Goodbye.

Thank you, Doctor. Goodbye, Miss Manton.

32 'The man at the hotel isn't Dr Manton. He has the same face, but he doesn't know Micky. Who is he?'

Hi, I'm Dr Eric Manton.

Hi, I'm Micky Munro.

33

Steve! Dr Manton is the 'wrong man'!

And Joan writes the letters! Let's find her! Quickly!

34 They find Joan Manton in her room. She can't move.

35 Steve and Sally help Joan Manton. She talks to them about the man. He isn't Dr Eric Manton.

Please help me! That man isn't my father – he's the killer!

36 Sally and Steve listen to Joan's story.

Two men kidnapped my father. One of them said to me, 'I'm now Dr Manton and you're my daughter'. I'm afraid of him. He has a gun.

37

The killer went with the bus to Uluru. Why?

He wants to kill Micky Munro because Micky knows about him.

Get the police, Sally! I'm going to find a helicopter.

Are you going to Uluru?

Yes – now!

Wait for me!

38 Steve is going to Uluru by helicopter. He wants to help Micky Munro and catch the killer. Sally is going to help Joan and her father.

Chapter 4

39 Uluru is in Uluru Park. Steve is talking to a park ranger about the people from the hotel.

The people from the hotel are climbing now. It's a long climb.

How can I go up quickly?

This is Jack, one of my men. He's a very quick climber.

Are you a good climber, Steve?

Yes, I am.

40 Jack, a park ranger, is going to take Steve up the Rock. He knows the Rock very well.

41 Steve and Jack are climbing up quickly.

You're good, Steve!

42 Steve sees the killer and Micky Munro. They're standing on the Rock, and there are no people near them. There's a strong wind.

43 The wrong Dr Manton wants to kill Micky Munro. He wants to kick him down the Rock. Micky is afraid.

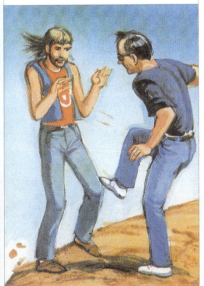

44 Steve hits the killer. The killer moves back and falls down the Rock.

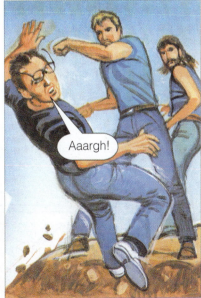

13

45 The killer is badly hurt. The rangers are going to take him to hospital. The police are coming. Now Steve wants to catch the boss of the gang.

48 Sally went with the police to Euralunga, an old house near Uluru. There was no problem. Joan's father, the 'right' Dr Eric Manton, was there and he wasn't hurt. Dr Manton is very happy because he's going to see his daughter again.

49 The Mantons and Micky Munro thank Sally and Steve. Micky is giving a concert in Sydney. He's going to send them tickets.

Thanks, Sally! Thanks, Steve, for your help! Come to my concert! I'm sending you tickets.

50 It's evening at the hotel. Steve and Sally are saying goodbye.

Thanks for your help, Sally.

That's OK. I've got a good story.

51

I'm going to Micky's concert. Are you coming with me, Sally?

Yes, of course.

I love you, Sally.

I love you, Steve.

15

ACTIVITIES

Before you read

1 Look at the pictures in the book. What is the story about?
2 Find the words in your dictionary. Write them in the sentences.

a *afraid gun hurt kidnapped kill*
A man ...... her. She was ...... , because he had a ....
But he didn't want to ...... her, and she wasn't ....

b *climb helicopter ranger rock wind*
The ...... is on a big .... He can't ..... down again,
because the ...... is very strong. A ...... is coming.

c *concert park manager singer*
A famous ...... is giving a ...... in the .... Her ...... is driving
her there.

d *boss Commissioner gang help hospital kicked*
A ...... of young men ...... the Police .... People in the
street didn't ...... him. He went to ...... , and now the police
have a new ....

After you read

3 Who are these people? Why are they important in the story?
   a Micky Munro   **b** Dr Manton   **c** Jack
4 Who is 'the wrong man'? Why was he 'the wrong man'?

Writing

5 Write Sally's story for her newspaper.
6 Are Steve and Sally going to meet again? What are they going to do? Write about it.